WELLINGTON'S WAR

A Living History

Young boys were used as bandsmen and deployed on the battlefield, playing music as the bullets flew.

DEDICATION

This book is dedicated to the soldiers and sailors of Britain, France and the rest of Europe who fought and died far from home. Also to the survivors who, often severely disabled, were forced to beg from the very people for whom they had fought. In war a hero, in peace a vagabond.

WELLINGTON'S WAR
A Living History

PAUL LEWIS ISEMONGER

FOREWORD BY RICHARD RUTHERFORD-MOORE

SUTTON PUBLISHING

First published in the United Kingdom in 1998
Sutton Publishing Ltd · Phoenix Mill · Far Thrupp · Stroud
Gloucestershire · GL5 2BU

British Library Cataloguing-in-Publication Data

ISBN 0-7509-1255-3

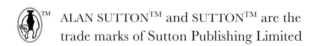

ALAN SUTTON™ and SUTTON™ are the
trade marks of Sutton Publishing Limited

Typeset in 11/14 pt Baskerville.
Typesetting and origination by
Sutton Publishing Limited.
Printed in Great Britain by
WBC Ltd, Bridgend.

CONTENTS

Foreword, by Richard Rutherford-Moore   vi

Acknowledgements   vii

Introduction   viii

Chronology   ix

1.   The Armies   1

2.   The Armies at War   11

3.   People at War   61

4.   Nelson's War   85

Useful Addresses   112

Re-enactment Groups   115

FOREWORD

The Royal Navy had enhanced its reputation already by the time the British Army landed in Portugal in 1808. It would be almost seven years before the 'redcoats' enjoyed a similar social standing to the 'bluejackets', years of struggle against heavy odds, with the political knife behind them at home, always drawn ready to be bloodied.

That the army achieved fame and fortune at this time is attributed to Arthur, Duke of Wellington. Despite the fact that before him the army had already been the instrument of successful land warfare and had enjoyed a limited success, under his leadership it would once again have the rest of Europe regarding it as they did in Marlborough's time, under his great captaincy.

Today 'Wellington's Army' has a similar following – tours, books, videos, lectures – so one can indulge oneself fully in the outpourings of many many past and present authors, presenters and spokesmen. Perhaps now it has almost reached the pinnacle of success – after all, imitation is the sincerest form of flattery!

Indulging myself in this way, and creating for myself the character of Rifleman Moore, led to an invitation to act as the Military and Technical Adviser on the *Sharpe* television series. In Bernard Cornwall's books, the men of Wellington's Army came alive and human for so many people for the first time – now we had the task of creating this sense of reality on the small screen for an even wider audience.

Rifleman Moore was born in the hard school of historical re-enactment in the 1970s and '80s. I learned my trade watching, learning and practising the skills which would enable me in the 1990s to train principal actors and over 2,000 extras on *Sharpe*.

This book tells in pictures and text the details of the military/naval war machines. You can get the benefit of many people's years of hard work, research and re-creation of their own particular interests in these enormous war-winning creations; the small cogs in the mechanism are generally of the most interest to re-enactors! Their expertise and Paul's sensitive photography make the book a *must* for any aspiring 'Napoleonic soldier', student or historian.

I had the good fortune to be inspired at an early age by the following people, whom I later came to know personally: Dr David G. Chandler, a constant support on *Sharpe*; Ian Fletcher, whose writings touched a nerve; Christopher Perko, whose devotion to the cause has led to the creation of a magnificent re-enactment group; Howard Giles, who has done more to promote the portrayal of military history through re-enactment than perhaps any other person in the United Kingdom; not to mention most of the people who have helped to re-create the scenes in this book.

Wellington's Army earned its place in history. By thought, talk and research, enthusiasts keep it alive. A student of the period cannot lose by an association with any of the groups featured in this book and will find a wealth of interesting detail within its pages – a truly 'living history'.

'Rifleman Moore' was killed at Waterloo, dressed as one of Napoleon's Imperial Guard in *Sharpe*. 'Pierced to the heart by Brown Bess', as Kipling wrote, it seemed a fitting end to my contribution towards this marvellous era of history. *Sharpe* inspired many with a deeper interest in Wellington's Army – but don't forget you have other senses besides your eyes. You must feel it, smell it and taste it to gain a full appreciation. The evocative and atmospheric images in this book will more than whet your appetite!

Richard Rutherford-Moore
11 November 1997
Written on the lower gundeck of HMS *Indefatigable*, filming *Hornblower*.

ACKNOWLEDGEMENTS

This book would not have been possible without the knowledgeable and enthusiastic help from many friends within the re-enactment world. To list them all would fill this entire book, so I hope you will forgive me if I select a few names to receive the laurels for all of you.

The proof-readers: Richard Rutherford-Moore, who also set up the rifles loading and firing sequence, Mike Freeman, Chris Jones, Chris Durkin, Wag Jones, Glen Robinson, Mike Grove, Keith Phillips.

Paul Meekins Books for supplying a constant stream of hard-to-find research material.

The Napoleonic Association, Les Handscombe, Norman Stringer, Malcolm MacDonald, John Wilson, Trevor Horn, Colin Ablett, Mark Dennis, Richard Ellis, The Trincomalee Trust, The Historical Maritime Society, Hartlepool Historic Quay (a flagship scheme of the Teesside Development Corporation), Dr H. Wills, Sharon Lockyer, Annie Blick, Joan and Marilyn.

INTRODUCTION

The smell of tar, wet hemp and salt-stained oak drifts across the sun-bleached deck of His Majesty's frigate *Trincomalee*. The freshening breeze sighs through the halyards as a tense silence grips the watchful seamen. The struggling prisoner is tied to the up-ended grating, his misdemeanours read out by a precise senior officer. Royal Marines stand stiffly either side of the bare-backed seaman, bayonets poised. The cat-o-nine-tails hisses through the air, its nine knotted lashes instantly drawing blood and muffled curses. Ten strokes later he is cut down and collapses face down on to the deck.

This is just one of the many 'Time-slips' that I have witnessed during the production of this book. There cannot be many photographers who have had the opportunity to stand in front of charging French cavalry, or beside a rank of British Redcoats as half of their number are cut down by a devastating musket volley, or witness the uncanny re-creation of Napoleon being greeted by his loyal torch-bearing troops against a golden sunset.

I hope that the following images will give you a glimpse of Wellington's War that is so masterfully re-created by a cast of thousands.

God Save the King, *Vivre l'Emperor*.

Paul Lewis Isemonger

CHRONOLOGY

1787
17 March. Arthur Wellesley commissioned as Ensign, 73rd Highlanders

1793
1 February. France declares war on Britain
14 April. British capture Tobago
28 June. Capture of Valenciennes by Allies
27 August. Occupation of Toulon by Anglo-Spanish Expedition
30 September. Arthur Wellesley commissioned Lieutenant-Colonel, 33rd Foot

1794
23 March. British capture Martinique
2 April. British capture St Lucia
21 April. British capture Guadeloupe
1 June. Admiral Howe defeats Villaret de Joyeuse on the 'Glorious 1 June'
15 September. Wellesley's first action at Boxtel in the Netherlands
10 December. The French recapture Guadeloupe

1795
14 April. Evacuation of British Netherlands expedition from Bremen
18 June. British leave St Lucia
16 August. British capture Cape of Good Hope

1796
5 February. Ceylon captured by the British
25 May. British re-occupy St Lucia
2 November. Franco-Spanish alliance forces British to evacuate Corsica
1 December. British leave Mediterranean

1797
14 February. Cordova defeated by Admiral Jervis at St Vincent
17 February. Trinidad captured by British
22–4 February. Unsuccessful French landing at Fishguard, Pembrokeshire
16–24 April. Spithead Mutiny
2 May–15 June. NORE Mutiny
11 October. Admiral Duncan defeats de Winter at Camperdown

1798
8 May. British re-enter Mediterranean
19 May. Unsuccessful British landing at Ostend
23 May. Rebellion in Ireland
12 June. Irish Rebels defeated at Vinegar Hill
1 August. French fleet comprehensively defeated by Nelson at Aboukir Bay
22 August. French expedition led by General Humbert lands at Killala Bay, Mayo
25 August. General Humbert defeats Lake at Castlebar
8 September. Cornwallis takes Humbert's surrender at Ballinamuck
15 November. Minorca captured by British
3 December. Income tax introduced to finance British war effort

1799
10 March. Sicily garrisoned by British troops
17 March. Acre besieged by Bonaparte

27 August. Anglo-Russian army lands in North Holland
19 September. 1st Battle of Bergen – Allies defeated
2 October. Anglo-Russians defeat French at 2nd Battle of Bergen
6 October. Allies defeated at Castricum
18 October. Convention of Alkmaar – Anglo-Russian army leaves North Holland

1800

21 January. Convention of El Arish between Anglo-Ottomans and French in Egypt. After repudiation of Convention, war starts again.
19 June. Unsuccessful British raid on Belle Isle
26 August. Unsuccessful British raid on Ferrol
5 September. Malta captured by British

1801

1 January. Act of Union between Britain and Ireland
8 March. British landing at Aboukir
21 March. Menou defeated by Abercromby at Alexandria
2 April. Danish fleet destroyed by Nelson at Copenhagen
27 June. Cairo captured by British
6 July. Sir James Saumarez fights inconclusive battle against French at Algeciras
12 July. Saumarez defeats Franco-Spanish fleet in 2nd Battle of Algeciras
2 September. French surrender in Egypt
1 October. Britain and France sign preliminary peace

1802

27 March. Peace of Amiens between France and Britain
29 April. Wellesley appointed Major-General

1803

16 May. Britain declares war on France
3 June. Hanover is captured by French
22 June. St Lucia is captured by British
30 June. Tobago is captured by British
11 August. Ahmednuggur is captured by Wellesley
20 September. Demerara captured by British
23 September. Wellesley is victorious at Assaye
29 November. Wellesley is victorious at Argaum
15 December. Wellesley captures Gawilghur

1804

5 May. Surinam captured by British
7 May. William Pitt becomes Prime Minister once again

1805

22 July. Villeneuve intercepted by Admiral Calder off Cape Finisterre
18 August. Villeneuve puts in to Cadiz
21 October. Villeneuve and the Franco-Spanish fleet are defeated off Cape Trafalgar
4 November. The remnants of the fleet are defeated off Rochefort

1806

8 January. Capetown captured by British
23 January. William Pitt dies
6 February. Defeat of Laissaque's French Squadron by Admiral Duckworth
12 May. Capri captured by British
17 June. British expedition to Buenos Ayres

4 July. Defeat of Reynier by Sir John Stuart at Maida in Calabria
8 October. Boulogne raided by Sydney Smith
21 November. Bonaparte proclaims blockade of Britain by Berlin Decrees

1807

7 January. Orders in Council in reply to Berlin Decrees
3 February. Montevideo captured by British
3 March. The attempt on the Dardanelles by the British is abandoned
17 March. British land in Egypt
28 June. British land at Buenos Ayres
5 July. Surrender of Whitelocke at Buenos Ayres
16 August. British land in Denmark
29 August. Wellesley defeats Danish army at Kjöge
7 September. Danish surrender
19 September. British withdrawn from Egypt
30 November. Lisbon occupied by French
17 December. Milan decree against Britain confirms the 'Continental System'

1808

1 August. British expedition disembarks in Portugal
17 August. Delaborde defeated by Wellesley at Roliça
21 August. Junot defeated by Wellesley at Vimeiro
30 August. Convention of Cintra
4 December. Napoleon enters Madrid. Moore retreats to Corunna

1809

16 January. Moore defeats Soult at Corunna
17 January. Moore's army evacuated
24 March. Martinique captured by British
11–12 April. French fleet attacked by Cochrane
22 April. Wellesley arrives in Portugal to command British forces
12 May. Wellesley forces the passage of the Douro at Oporto
6 July. Wellesley appointed Marshal-General of Portugal
27–8 July. Victory for Wellesley at Talavera
30 July. British land at Walcheren
4 September. Wellesley becomes Viscount Wellington of Talavera and Wellington
20 October. Wellington starts the building of the Lines of Torres Vedras
9 December. Walcheren evacuated by British

1810

4 February. British capture Guadeloupe
17 February. British capture Amboyna
23–8 August. British naval defeat at Ile de France
27 September. Wellington defeats Massena at Busaco
10 October. Massena halted by lines of Torres Vedras
2 December. British capture Ile de France

1811

4 March. Graham's victory at Barrosa
13 March. Hoste defeats Franco-Italian naval force off Lissa
3 April. French evacuate Portugal
3–5 May. Wellington defeats Massena at Fuentes de Onoro
16 May. Beresford defeats Soult at Albuera
18 September. Java captured by British

1812

19 January. Wellington captures Ciudad Rodrigo
6 April. Badajoz captured by Wellington
11 May. Prime Minister Spencer Perceval assassinated
19 June. USA declares war on Britain
22 July. Wellington defeats Marmont at Salamanca
12 August. Wellington enters Madrid
16 August. British capture Detroit
18 August. Wellington becomes Marquess
17 September. Burgos beseiged by Wellington
13 October. American invasion of Canada defeated at Queenston
19 November. Wellington returns to Portugal

1813

4 March. Wellington appointed a Knight of the Garter
24 April. Americans burn York (Toronto)
23 May. British troops led into Spain by Wellington
28–9 May. British defeated by Americans at Sackets Harbor
1 June. HMS *Shannon* captures USS *Chesapeake*
21 June. Wellington defeats Joseph Bonaparte at Vittoria
26 July–1 August. Wellington defeats Soult
31 August. Wellington captures San Sebastian
10 September. British squadron defeated by Americans on Lake Erie
5 October. British defeated by Americans at the Battle of the Thames
7 October. Wellington forces the passage of the Bidassoa and France is invaded
25 October. Americans defeated at Battle of Chateaugay
10 November. Soult defeated by Wellington
11 November. Americans defeated at Chrysler's Farm
10–13 December. Wellington defeats Soult on the Nive

1814

27 February. Soult defeated at Orthez
12 March. Wellington enters Bordeaux
10 April. Wellington defeats Soult at Toulouse four days after Napoleon's abdication
11 May. Wellington becomes Duke
5 July. British defeated by Americans at Chipewa
25 July. Americans defeated at Lundy's Lane
24 August. Americans defeated at Bladensburg
24–5 August. Washington burnt by British
12–14 September. Unsuccessful British attack on Baltimore
13 December. British expedition arrives at New Orleans
24 December. Treaty of Ghent brings peace between Britain and USA

1815

8 January. British attack on New Orleans fails
1 March. Napoleon returns to France
15 June. Napoleon invades the Netherlands
16 June. Wellington defeats Ney at Quatre Bras; Napoleon defeats Blücher at Ligny
17 June. Wellington withdraws to Mont St Jean
18 June. Wellington and Blücher defeat Napoleon at Waterloo
22 June. Napoleon abdicates
7 July. Wellington and Blücher enter Paris

SECTION ONE
The Armies

The British Infantry

9th (East Norfolk) Regiment of Foot at the time of the Peninsular Campaign. This infantryman is wearing the 'stovepipe' shako, a type of cap used throughout the campaign.

42nd Royal Highland Regiment.

In 1815 at Quatre Bras the 42nd Royal Highland Regiment were overrun by cavalry, with the loss of 314 men and 24 officers. Absorbing these near catastrophic losses they marched onto the field of Waterloo a mere two days later.

The French Infantry

21ème de ligne, *c.* 1815. This regiment can trace its beginnings back to 1589 and still exists in the 1990s. The 'Premier Porte Aigle' holds the Eagle.

The Infantryman in full campaign kit.

A column of French Infantry with the Tambour (drummer).

The British Cavalry

The British cavalry was divided into the Light Dragoons, the Household Cavalry and the Heavy Cavalry. The Hussars, pictured here, were to all intents and purposes Light Dragoons in all but name and uniform. There were four Hussar regiments.

The Hussar uniform had a distinctive look with a fur-trimmed jacket, worn apparently casually over the shoulder. The cap was a distinctive red shako.

The British cavalry did not play a large role in the wars until the Peninsular Campaign when the terrain was suitable for cavalry tactics.

The 12th Light Dragoons, the equivalent of the Light Infantry. Unlike the Dragoons of previous centuries they were unlikely to dismount and fight on foot. In general the Light Dragoons acted as skirmishers and scouts, while still being able to mount the shock attacks so typical of cavalry.

The French Cavalry

The French divided their cavalry into light and heavy. Left: 1er Regiment de Chasseurs à Cheval de ligne. The workhorse line cavalry often fought beside the infantry.

The Artillery

Britain's artillery force was meagre in comparison to its enemies' vast array of field weapons. This state of affairs lasted throughout the war.

The Armies at War

The Cavalry

The cavalry fought mostly at close range – basic and bloody.

12th Prince of Wales Light Dragoons. Their uniform is based on the French style, often leading to confusion for both sides.

The 12th at La Belle Alliance, Waterloo.

The training that British cavalry troops received at home bore little resemblance to the realities of the conditions and requirements of war in a foreign land. Parade ground manoeuvres could not be applied to battlefields, rendering newly assigned units of little use until broken in to the ways of war.

British Life Guards. Heavy Cavalry. They, and other senior regiments of the Heavy Cavalry, were known as the Household Cavalry. Theoretically they only took the field in the presence of the King. In fact the Life Guards did not see action until 1812 when they were sent to the Peninsular Campaign.

The French cavalry was organized into the 'Light' and 'Heavy' regiments. These Chasseurs formed part of the Light Cavalry.

Less flamboyant than the French Hussars, but just as effective, the Chasseurs à Cheval often adopted items of Hussar uniform.

THE LIGHT CAVALRY SABRE

The curved light cavalry sabre was an effective weapon against either infantry or cavalry. The action was either a swinging cut, the curvature of the blade slicing through cloth and flesh, or a thrust, the sharp point penetrating deeply or even 'running through' an opponent.

The French light cavalry sabre.

The correct balanced grip.

From the vantage point of the saddle the correctly handled sabre was an awesome weapon, with a wide arc of effectiveness, as demonstrated here by a British cavalryman.

French Light Cavalry. Common to all cavalry was the ability to demoralize infantry with thundering frontal charges.

Saddlery of the French Chasseurs à Cheval.

The British Infantry

An officer wearing the bicorn hat in the style of the period.

The knapsack weighed about 30 lb (15 kg), had a wooden frame and was made from tarred canvas. Generally speaking it was used to carry spare clothes and cleaning equipment. The frame made it highly uncomfortable and the cross straps constricted the chest.

The entire personal equipment weighed about 60 lb (30 kg) dry. In wet weather the weight carried would be considerably more due to the absorbency of the woollen and canvas uniform. A greatcoat was worn in bad weather. Also made of wool this too would increase in weight the wetter it got. Many men died of exhaustion on long marches. The plus side was that, wet or dry, the clothes kept the soldier warm.

The stock was a hard leather strap worn around the neck. Its purpose was to keep the chin up. This was achieved at the cost of frequent sores and infections caused by the chafing of the leather.

Short buttoned gaiters.

The woollen tunic.

The wooden water bottle was also carried on a strap behind the bayonet.

The soldier was paid 1s per day, half of which was deducted for 'prog', his food ration. As well as deductions for food, each soldier had to part with 4d per week for washing clothes. Each year 4s and 4d was deducted for whitening and pipe clay to keep the white leatherwork bright, 1s 3d for shoe brushes, 2s for blackball to blacken equipment, 4s to have his boots soled and heeled and every two years 1s for a clothes brush, plus other payments including one day's pay per year for the upkeep of hospitals for old and incapacitated soldiers at Chelsea and Kilmainham. If any of the equipment was lost it had to be paid for.

The French Infantry

Fantasin. French infantryman of the 21ème de ligne, 1812–15.

'Butin' was a colloquial expression for personal kit. It was the origin of the word 'booty', used to describe captured equipment.

The shako was a cap made with a leather peak and reinforcing bands, a metal plate with the regimental number, cockade, and chin strap.

Introduced for light troops in the 1790s, the shako had become standard by 1808.

The knapsack (*sac à dos*) was made from hide with the hair left on the skin, facing outwards.

The greatcoat is seen rolled in a linen sack on top of the *sac à dos*.

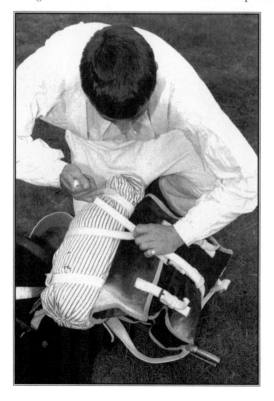

The coat was secured to the *sac à dos* by at first two then three straps.

The cartridge box (*giberne*) was worn over the left shoulder beneath the epaulette. It carried thirty-five rounds.

A white linen cover was put over the black leather cartridge box.

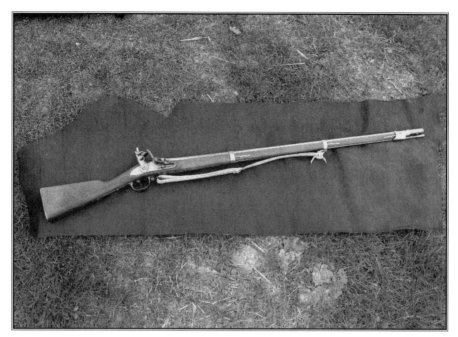

The 'Charleville' M.1777 French musket. It was named after the place where first manufactured.

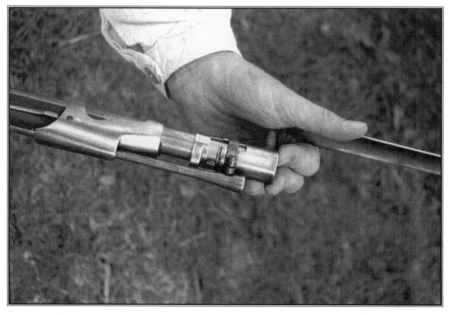

Method of bayonet attachment.

The bayonet was 406 mm long.

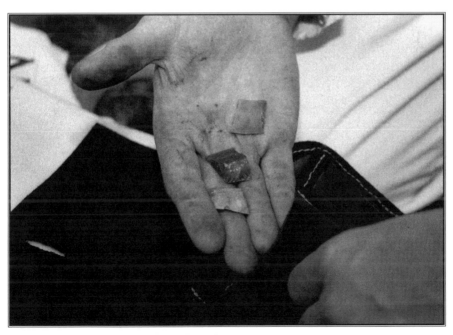

Flints (*silex*) for the lock of the flintlock musket.

Woollen jacket (*habit veste*).

Overalls (*pantalons de toile*).

Shorter gaiters (*guetres*) were worn after 1812.

French Infantry Fusilier of the 45ème de ligne of the period 1808–9 (this page and opposite).

Note the longer gaiters.

THE LOADING AND FIRING SEQUENCE OF THE FLINTLOCK MUSKET

1. With the frizzen forward the pan is open and ready to receive the priming powder. The cock holding the flint is put to 'half cock'. This put the weapon into a safe state where the mechanism could not be operated if the trigger was accidently knocked.

2. A greased paper cartridge containing the lead musket ball and a measured charge of gunpowder is removed from the cartridge box. The top of the cartridge is bitten off.

3. The soldier tips a small quantity of the powder into the open pan.

4. The powder in the pan.

5. The pan is closed.

6. The rest of the powder is tipped into the barrel, followed by the paper cartridge containing the ball. Later in the war veteran soldiers 'turned' the cartridge after charging the barrel and inserted the ball end first, tearing off the excess paper – the result was more accuracy as the ball did not have a 'burning comet's tail' attached to it.

7. The ramrod is removed from its storage place beneath the barrel.

8. The steel ramrod is reversed and the wider end is placed into the muzzle of the barrel.

9. The whole charge is rammed home. This compression is an essential part of loading. If the powder is not sufficiently compressed it will not explode but merely flare with severely diminished propulsive force, at best just bruising the enemy. Note how the bayonet is angled outwards to prevent the soldier impaling his hand as he rammed home the bullet.

10. The ramrod is withdrawn and reversed . . .

11. . . . before being replaced in the holder beneath the barrel.

12. The soldier waits for the order to fire.

13. 'Give fire!'

14. The lead ball exits the barrel at over 500 miles per hour.

British 'Chosen Man' of the 9th East Norfolk Regiment of Foot.

The priming pan is opened by pushing forward the hinged striking plate known as the frizzen.

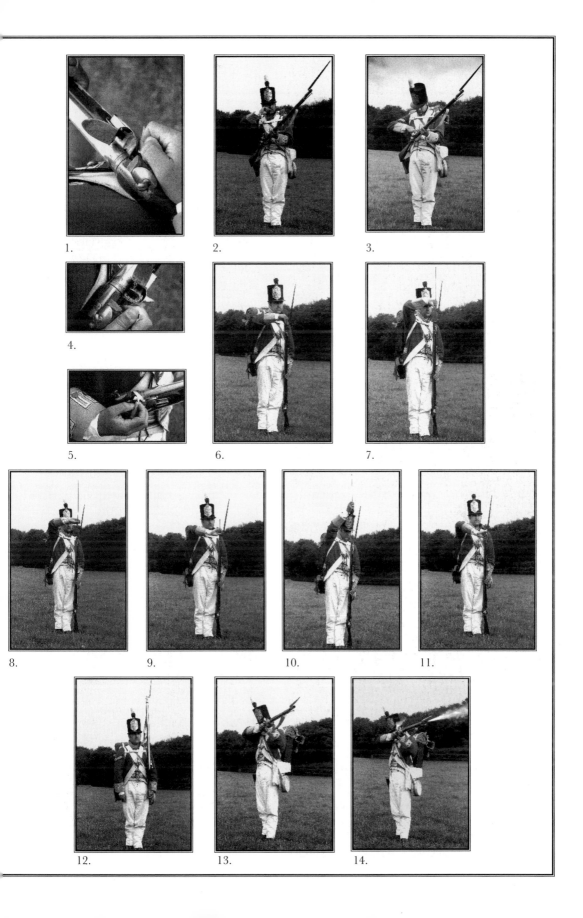

1.

2.

3.

4.

5.

6.

7.

8.

9.

10.

11.

12.

13.

14.

Infantry Tactics

The defensive square. Anything from 150 to 200 infantry formed one side of the square. As

casualties rose the square would become progressively smaller.

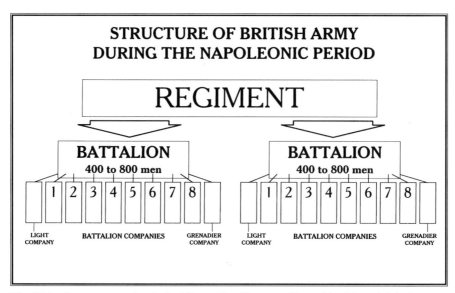

The Light Company consisted of soldiers of intelligence, able to skirmish and fight in an unregimented style. Grenadiers were the élite troops, thought to be the bravest and sent into the thick of the action.

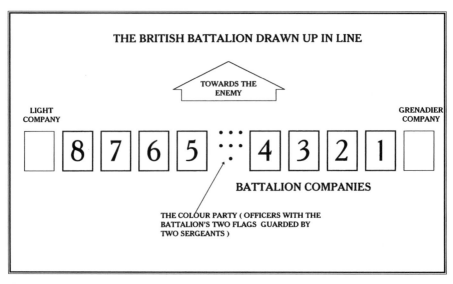

The structure of a British battalion line.

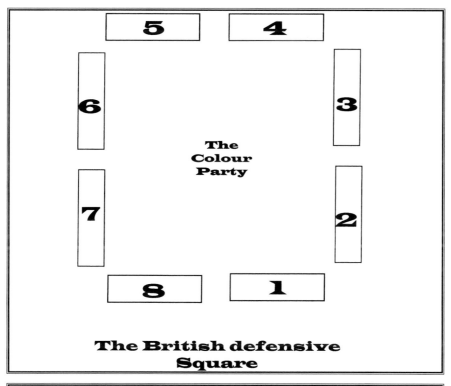

The British defensive Square

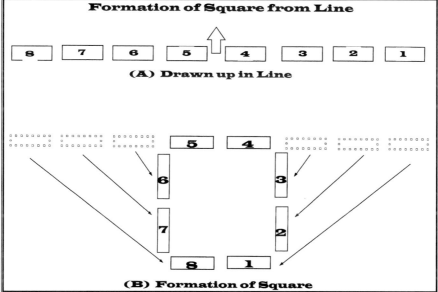

Formation of Square from Line

(A) Drawn up in Line

(B) Formation of Square

When in open country the Line was vulnerable to attack from cavalry, either from the rear or the side (flank). To counter this danger a square could quickly be formed, giving all-round protection. Officers, the band, colour party and pioneers would form up in the centre of the protecting square.

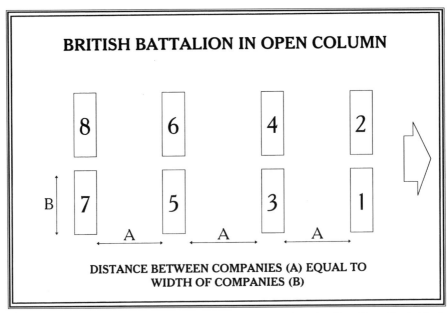

BRITISH BATTALION IN OPEN COLUMN

8   6   4   2

B   7   5   3   1

A   A   A

DISTANCE BETWEEN COMPANIES (A) EQUAL TO
WIDTH OF COMPANIES (B)

The column was the standard formation for manoeuvring the Battalion. Each block represents a company. Close column was formed by the distance 'A' being shortened by two paces. This was not a fighting formation.

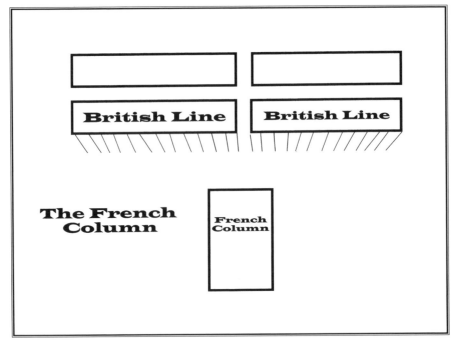

British Line   British Line

The French Column   French Column

The British were able to concentrate fire on the tightly packed French Column. The French used the column as both a manoeuvring and a fighting formation

From the early days of the wars the French favoured the column as a form of attack, one
reason being that the massive army assembled by Napoleon would at any one time consist
of a high proportion of new recruits who would have been unable to execute the complex
field manoeuvres needed for line and square formation. This system had its drawbacks. As
the French engaged the British, who were drawn up in two ranks, they presented a dense
target and were not able to respond with the full force of the available muskets. Only the
front and sides could bring their guns to bear without endangering fellow Frenchmen.

Napoleon presented each regiment with an Eagle standard. This symbol became the embodiment of the soul of the regiment. To lose an Eagle was the worst fate that could befall the fighting men. Consequently the Eagles were the prize that all British Redcoats sought.

The British 87th Foot captured an Eagle at Barrosa from the élite 8th Grenadier Battalion, as this contemporary report in *Bells Weekly Messenger* illustrated.

FRENCH EAGLE.

"*Isla de Leon*, March 7, 1811.

"At four o'clock on the 4th we got orders to move on, and marched 16 hours without halting. As we were passing through a wood the General received an express that the French were formed on the hill to our right to give us battle; we came to the right about, and met them with the impetuosity of lions. Their force consisted of 11,000 men, under the command of Victor, Duke of Belluno. The Spaniards had previously left us, and were at the distance of four miles, destroying the French encampments and works opposite Point St. Peire. We then drew out our light brigade, the 95th rifle corps, the 2d hussars, King's German Legion, and our flank battalions, to cover our formation as we left the wood. We now formed independent lines, under the hottest and most galling fire of large shot, shell, grape, canister, and musketry, that ever was seen or felt in the annals of war. The French advanced close to our front, beating the *pas de charge*. The Prince's Irish were formed at this time, and at ordered arms; they lost one Major, one Captain, four Lieutenants, one Ensign, and one hundred rank and file, before we shouldered; for if we attempted to fire, we should inevitably destroy our own light troops, who were performing deeds of valour: being overpowered by numbers, they were obliged to fall back. We proceeded to take up the position they quitted; 1000 of the brave Guards, and the 67th on our right, the 28th, and remainder of the 2d and 3d Guards, nearly the same number, on our left; we kept up an immense fire for two hours, with great slaughter on both sides; our ammunition was nearly exhausted, when we gave three cheers, and brave Graham cried out—"Charge with the bayonet," which they got in fine style.

"The 87th charged the 8th Grenadier French battalion, the pride of France, and am happy to say, we took their two howitzers, and wreathed the Eagle in the charge, a glory never before atchieved by any regiment in the world. All the other regiments had their Eagles screwed on, in order to take them off when hard pushed, but Bonaparte ordered the 8th, 1600 grenadiers, to nail theirs on, as he said it was impossible to take it; but, thank God, a Roscommon man took it, one of my volunteers (Masterson), who was the right hand man of Captain Roper's company, in which I was, when in that regiment. I had him made serjeant about two years ago, and am now happy to say, I saw him promoted to the rank of serjeant-major on the field of battle. The French lost near 4,000 men, and our little army, I am sorry to state, lost the third part of their force. I herewith send you a return of our killed and wounded. I cannot conclude without expressing my unfeigned regret for the loss of poor Keogh, an Ensign of ours, who was shot through the heart, in the act of seizing the Eagle with Masterson.—I am, your affectionate Brother,

"T. D. without a wound."

The 95th Rifles

Defined as a light infantry regiment, the Rifles became one of the most respected and proficient regiments of the Napoleonic wars.

Their uniform was dark green with black facings and white piping. The cap was the light infantry 'stovepipe' shako. They carried the Baker rifle, highly accurate for the time.

The Rifle Corps were usually the first to give and receive fire in a confrontation, skirmishing ahead of the main army, using cover wherever possible. This was a radical departure from the usual tactics of lines of troops with their well-disciplined but mechanical line movements. Riflemen were allowed to be individuals while still fighting as a group.

Fleetness of foot and above average intelligence were among the requirements for riflemen.

The Baker rifle was a highly efficient and formidable weapon. The bore of the barrel was cut with a series of spiral grooves. This caused the bullet to spin as it was fired, making its trajectory highly accurate. It was designed by London gunsmith Ezekiel Baker. The barrel was 30 in, short when compared to the longer musket.

The following sequence shows one method of loading and firing. The first stage in firing it was to remove lock cap and tompion (used to protect the vulnerable lock and to prevent water and dirt from entering the barrel). Then 'open' lock, clear vent and wipe steel face of frizzen (to ensure a dry surface for the flint to strike sparks).

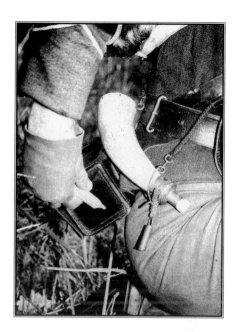

Take a cartridge from the box.

Bite off the bullet, or
alternatively cut the paper
across the sharp gunflint.

Charge the barrel with powder, then throw down the empty cartridge.

Remove the paper from the bullet. The bullet was wrapped in a greased leather patch to make a tight fit in the barrel and hence a more accurate result. Note the rifling of the barrel.

Place the ball onto the bore with thumb and 'start' the ball with the flat end of the ramrod. The Baker ramrod had a swell near the 'flat' end to facilitate this method.

ush ball home to powder with ramrod.

Prime the lock with flask or horn.

Rifle is now ready to fire, after adjusting for target. The Baker was capable of hitting a man at distances up to 250 yd. During simulations even greater ranges have been achieved.

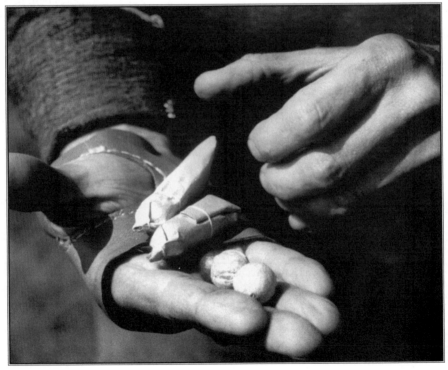

Facsimiles of cartridges and original leather-covered bullets.

The Horn badge worn on the shako denoted that the Rifles were a light infantry corps.

Regular cleaning of any firearm was essential to prevent a misfire or 'flash in the pan'. The black powder was coarse and produced by-products when ignited that would soon block the touch-hole or barrel.

On occasion the powder would not fire, leaving a full charge plus a ball in the barrel. This was remedied by using a ball-puller.

This ball-puller was placed down the barrel and twisted so that the screw-thread spike would pierce the soft lead ball and allow it to be withdrawn. The faulty charge could then be tipped out and the loading procedure repeated. To achieve the torque required to pull the ball out, a 'tommy bar' was fitted through the hole in the 'flat' end of the ramrod.

After a battle the burnt by-products had to be removed from the rifle. This was best achieved by pouring boiling water into the muzzle of the weapon, cleaning both bore and the small touch-hole.

Water exiting the touch-hole.

Artillery

A number of types of artillery were in use by the British during the wars with France. The various types and calibres were used for different purposes: siege, garrison, coastal defence, naval and field guns. They ranged in type from howitzers to carronades and mortars. Many of the guns, particularly the ones made of brass, became obsolete during this period, often because of repeated failure in the testing conditions of the Peninsular War.

In 1793 the Royal Horse Artillery was formed. All artillery officers were well schooled in the theory and practice of the gunner's art, or rather science.

Unlike other sections of the army, artillery officers could not purchase their commissions and any promotion was as a result of seniority.

FIRING A CANNON

Round shot was by far the most common form of projectile. This solid iron ball cast to an exact size for a particular type of gun had the furthest range of all projectiles. One of the most effective ways of using round shot against troops was to fire the ball so that it bounced on the ground (grazed) in front of them. It would then ricochet into the massed ranks creating numerous casualties. The ball would cause injury almost until it finally ran out of momentum. A fast-rolling ball was quite capable of taking off a foot. One round shot could account for the loss of 20–30 men. Round shot could also be heated until it glowed red. When fired it could start fires in a besieged town or on the decks of a ship.

1. The barrel is 'sponged out' with a piece of wet sheepskin attached to the end of a pole. This ensures any smouldering remnants from the last firing are extinguished.

2. The ventsman places his thumb over the touch-hole (usually in a leather stall) to prevent ingress of air and potential blowback of unfired powder at the spongeman.

3. A cartridge made of paper, flannel or serge and containing gun powder is placed in the muzzle followed by the projectile (in this case round shot). The ball and powder were often wrapped together to speed the loading process. The ball was smaller than the bore of the barrel; this difference in size was called 'windage'. The tighter the fit the more accurate the shot.

4. The cartridge and ball are rammed in with the reverse end of the sponge. To obtain better powder compression, and hence a more efficient explosion, wads of straw, dry grass or sods of earth were rammed on top.

5. The ventsman then inserts a 'pricker', a long thin spike, into the touch-hole to pierce the cartridge and expose the gunpowder.

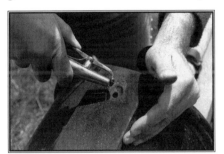

6. Several methods of priming were used during the Napoleonic era: fine powder in a quill or paper tube was inserted into the touch-hole; a length of quickmatch (strands of cotton soaked in saltpetre and spirits of wine) were inserted; or, as illustrated, fine powder was dispensed from a powder horn into the conical depression at the top of the touch-hole.

7. The touch-hole is covered by the ventsman.

8. The order, 'Give fire!'

9. A 'portfire' holding a length of smouldering 'slow-match' is applied to the touch-hole.

10. The powder ignites, . . .

11. . . . firing the main charge.

Used on both land and sea, the rocket was a paper (later metal) tube filled with gunpowder. Rocket sizes were divided into heavy, medium and light. The largest were 8 in in diameter. A specialist British Rocket Troop was formed in 1814. The purpose of the rockets was to cause fires or to carry explosives timed with a fuse. The trajectory was somewhat unpredictable.

As this contemporary report from the *London Chronicle* of March 1814 indicates, rockets had a demoralizing effect on the enemy. Unlike musket balls and cannon shot, the soldiers could see the rocket coming

ROCKETS—PASSAGE OF THE ADOUR.

EXTRACT OF A LETTER FROM AN OFFICER IN LORD WELLINGTON'S ARMY.

" In my last, I informed you that the Rocket Brigade was to be employed in the crossing of the Adour. Forty artillerymen were accordingly ordered, and carried with them one hundred and sixty rounds ; one round of which was carried by hand, and the remaining ones in the pouches for that purpose. They marched from Bidart in the evening of the 22d, under the command of Capt. Lane, of the Artillery, and arrived, with the Brigades of Guards, close to the mouth of the harbour before daylight. The pontoons not having all arrived, it was impossible to throw a bridge across. About ten or eleven o'clock, some of the light infantry of the Coldstream and 3d Guards got across in small boats, which they continued to do, unmolested, till about half-past four, or perhaps five o'clock ; when the enemy made their appearance, in number about two thousand, in two columns, and a small one on their right. The rocketeers were immediately sent over, and arrived just at a *proper* and *happy moment.* The positions for two batteries of twenty rockets were directly taken up, and most part of them sent off rapidly after one another, at a distance of about three hundred yards. The enemy gave way, and ran. Directly on this, the rocket party advanced on the left, in ' *double quick,*' occasionally firing a few to accelerate their flight. The light infantry of the Guards, rapidly advancing, regained the heights they had been driven from. The rocket battery still advanced beyond their front, and fired a few more rounds. *The enemy ran most manfully.* The force of the enemy was so greatly superior to ours, that the party of the Guards at that time across the Adour, not exceeding 600 men, must have suffered very severely ; and the passage for the other divisions and troops must have been much procrastinated. Thousands of troops were present on the other bank of the river, who witnessed the instantaneous effect the rockets produced on the enemy. Their reputation is now firmly established with those divisions who saw them used.

" Only three companies of the Guards were engaged, not more than 250 men, these and forty artillerymen, armed with rockets, *put to flight* 2000 men.

" Had we had one hour's more day light it is probable the greatest part of the enemy's column would have been cut up.

" I saw in one place seven Frenchmen killed and wounded by one rocket, and in another spot four. We buried 33 within our lines, and the peasants report their loss in killed and wounded to be 400, this, I think, must be exaggerated ; however, they suffered severely, and we have heard of several officers being killed and wounded since the affair.

People at War

Many first-hand accounts have come down to the present day from both officers and ordinary soldiers in the form of diaries and letters.

Cantinière, a French sutleress. Although women did not fight in the war, many travelled with the armies, some as wives and some as servants, sutlers, or prostitutes.

In the British Army 6 wives were permitted per company of 100 men while stationed at home. Of course these numbers were often exceeded, leading to distressing times if the regiment was ordered overseas and the quota was strictly enforced.

The dismissed wife of the ordinary soldier was given a pass that entitled her to food and accommodation as she walked the many miles back to her home. She then faced the prospect of an indeterminate period without her companion or any financial support.

Officers

Cavalry officer and his batman. Officers in the British Army were drawn from the landed gentry and frequently paid for their commission.

A French Company officer (Lieutenant) of 21ème de ligne, 1812–15. Field officer rank (i.e. any rank above captain) was denoted by lace on the shako, shoulder epaulettes and a half-moon-shaped gorget worn around the neck. The gorget was common to both French and British officers. It was a scaled-down, purely decorative descendant of the piece of neck armour worn by officers in the seventeenth century.

Sergeant (NCO). The French Army had lost most of its regular officers after the Revolution and was ill prepared for the Emperor's desire to conquer Europe. Gradually this changed and a whole generation of leaders was formed in the heat of battle. NCOs (Non-Commissioned Officers) were often propelled into the ranks of the officers. Generally speaking these officers were more likely to come from the same social class as the men and therefore engendered their respect rather than fear, which was the British method.

British Infantry Officers.

Non-Commissioned Officers

The 'Chosen Man' (Lance Corporal) of the 42nd Royal Highland Regiment.

A Corporal of the 9th (East Norfolk) Regiment of Foot. There were three corporals to each Company.

The Sergeant. Each Company had two sergeants.

Each regiment of any of the participating nations had its own drummers. They served several purposes: they could signal the various battlefield manoeuvres to the infantry and stiffen the resolve of the men.

Because of their importance they became, along with the officers, prime targets for marksmen to 'pick off'.

The sword would rarely be used in anger.

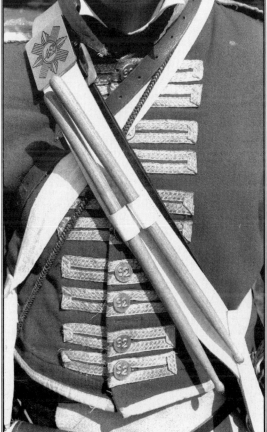

Drumsticks attached to the cross-belt.

Pipers led the Highland Regiments into battle.

British Recruitment and Army Life

The reality of army life was wretched by today's standards. The allocated barrack living-space was half that of a convict. Low pay and a very low level of respect among the general population forced the army into devious ways to maintain a serviceable army.

Recruiting parties were sent out to villages and towns where they would set up a colourful display in the local hostelries. Drums would beat and fifes would play a stirring tune as the friendly sergeant talked of past glorious victories and the benefits of army life, with the prospect of rapid promotion. Alcohol flowed freely and the unwary young men were encouraged to drink by the publican who received a payment for each signed-up soldier. When the time was right and the senses dulled the *coup-de-gras* was applied in the form of an offer of money: 12 guineas for just a signature. Many took the bounty with little thought beyond such comparative wealth. Their fantasy was soon dashed when they awoke to find themselves legally a soldier in His Majesty's Army. From their promised bounty £2 14s was deducted for their 'necessaries'. This kit comprised cloth gaiters, two pairs of shoes, one pair of stockings (or two pairs of socks), two shirts, a foraging cap, a pair of worsted mittens and a knapsack. If the new recruit did not drink away his bounty he was the exception. Army life, far from being a way to fortune, often started in debt.

It is an astonishing fact that these underhand methods and an unpleasant life in the army produced an army of Redcoats that became highly respected by foreign armies. Wellington said of his men that they were 'The scum of the earth . . . it is really wonderful that we should have made them the fine fellows they are.'

British soldiers were recruited from the age of eighteen. This was lowered to fourteen in 1805, although these young men were put into a holding camp until old enough to fight. Young inexperienced soldiers were called 'Johnny Newcombe'.

In France any male between the ages of eighteen and twenty-five was liable to be conscripted into service. The maximum age was later raised to thirty.

Supplies

The Commissaire de Guerre was responsible for supplying the French Army. Throughout the Napoleonic period the French Army received its food from foraging and forced requisition. This resulted in a significant strategic advantage; an army living off the land was not tied to supply depots and supply lines and was therefore more manoeuvrable. Other essentials such as ammunition and footwear were brought to the army by private contractors. These civilians were prone to even more corruption than the army and eventually the system failed entirely. Napoleon formed the military 'Train des Equipages' consisting of eight battalions of four companies with about 140 wagons each. This number increased during the war, although the supply problem was never satisfactorily resolved.

The British infantry soldier received good if somewhat basic food. The daily rations included 1lb of meat (including bone), 1½lb of bread (known as Brown George) and a quart of beer.

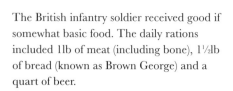

The meat was often made into a thin watery soup called 'skilly' or a simple stew called 'stirabout'.

The two daily meals were prepared by each man in turn, one in the morning and one at midday.

Island Defence

After England declared war on France in 1803 Bonaparte concentrated three army corps of veteran soldiers along the French coast between Calais and Etaples, known as the Camp of Boulogne. The intent of invasion was obvious. Flat-bottomed barges were ordered to be built along with a multitude of smaller craft. Within two years Napoleon had sufficient shipping for 168,000 troops.

Fears grew in England that Napoleon might be able to gain control over the narrow straits between France and England for a sufficient period of time to allow his invasion fleet to cross. If the French could land and march across English fields it seemed that the war might soon be over. Coastal defence became paramount.

In 1803 Captain William Ford proposed strengthening existing earthwork fortifications with a chain of gun towers along the Sussex and Kent coasts. Each tower would be equipped with a large single gun able to project an unbroken protection of crossfire across the inshore waters. With some modifications his idea was accepted. The main armament was a single 24-pounder gun mounted on a carriage able to traverse through 360°.

This form of defence was not new to the military. In 1794 Lord Hood, with a fleet of warships, was sent to capture Corsica. One single watch tower at Martello Point, armed only with one 6-pounder and two 18-pounder guns, repulsed an attack by HMS *Juno* and HMS *Fortitude* with a combined armament of 101 guns. Both ships were forced to withdraw with serious casualties and damage. The tower only surrendered after two days of continuous bombardment by a four-gun battery built only 150 yd from the tower! William Ford's towers became known as Martello Towers.

The Edinburgh Evening Courant
October 23rd 1809

FORTIFICATIONS.—The works erected on that part of the coast of Kent, which cannot be considered under the protection of our shipping in the Downs, are now nearly completed ; they begin with the ancient castle of Dover, which, from its peculiar strength and elevated situation, has long been considered impregnable. Government have, however, been employed in constructing subterraneous works, consisting of three tiers of batteries, casemates, &c. with barracks for 10,000 men. The height opposite the barracks is also regularly fortified by flanking redoubts, bastions, &c. There is also a citadel with ditch and drawbridge, and barracks for 5000 men ; a shaft, of a most beautiful and commodious description, having four different staircases (round an open area which both lights and ventilates) communicates with the town, the height of which is upwards of 300 feet. By this shaft it is calculated that 20,000 men might pass from the height to the town, or *vice versa*, in half an hour. There are also four other batteries, called Guildford's, Townshend's, Amherst's, and Archcliffe. From Dover to Folkstone no works of defence are necessary, as the cliff is inaccessible. From Folkestone to Dungeness, forming an open bay of twenty miles in breadth, a great number of martello towers are constructed, which are of a circular form, bomb proof, and have one gun, of very large calibre, on the top ; they are so distributed that no part of the coast which is assailable is without the range of their shot ; 30 men in each might defend themselves as long as their provisions lasted. The old castle of Sandgate has also been greatly enlarged, and now contains a number of guns. A redoubt, consisting of bomb proof towers and very formidable outworks, has also been erected at Brockman's Barn. At Shorncliffe there is a battery, called by that name ; and at Hythe, Sutherland, and Moncrief, batteries which, with three others at Dungeness, complete the line of coast. In addition to the above, a military canal has been cut from Shorncliffe to near Rye. Much difference of opinion has arisen as to the utility of this canal, as a defensive military work ; but thus much is certain, that it opens an easy communication with a part of the country called the Wold or Wild of Kent, which, from the badness of its roads, and consequent difficulty of getting its produce (consisting of timber) to market, has been cut off from intercourse with the rest of the county, and which this canal will most effectually obviate. It also begins to be of the most essential service for the conveyance of troops and baggage, many regiments having passed from Rye to Hythe, a distance of 25 miles, without fatigue ; and immediately after landing, a distance of fifteen miles farther by land, without halting, thereby performing a distance of forty miles in one day, saving a great expence to Government, and relieving the innkeepers, who are very thinly scattered in that neigbourhood, from an oppressive burden.

The whole of the works above described are performed in the most substantial and skilful manner, and display great science in the engineer department. It is also matter of pleasing reflection, that many of the roads, canals, &c. unite great commercial advantages with vast defensive preparations.

WILLIAM HOBSON
BUILDER OF MANY OF THE
SOUTH COAST MARTELLO TOWERS

Martello towers.

Each tower had only one entrance built on the shore side. Access was by a single ladder which could be drawn up. The walls were thickest on the side facing seawards.

The towers were manned by Artillery Volunteers, mostly recruited from the local area and strengthened by regulars of the Royal Artillery.

The basement storage was used for ammunition and provisions.

The stairway built into the thick wall led from the gun platform to the soldiers' quarters.

The musket rack was built around the central pillar in the men's quarters.

Royal Military Canal

In 1804 Lieutenant-Colonel John Brown suggested a plan for a defensive canal along the Sussex and Kent coasts. The idea was to build a waterway from Shorncliffe near Folkstone to the River Rother near Rye, some 19 miles. Before construction started it was suggested that the canal be taken from the River Rother to Pett Level, 3 miles east of Hastings, making the total length 28 miles, 22½ of which had to be dug. A road was to be built alongside, which would be screened by a parapet built from the soil dug out of the canal. A secondary purpose to the line of defence would be the facilitation of troop movements along the canal or road.

Although the first sections of the canal at the eastern end were the required width of 62 ft, as the construction progressed the team of navigators, or navvies (the diggers), came across increasing problems and the width over the majority of the canal was only half that required. Whether or not this narrow strip of water would have repulsed Napoleon's mighty army remained theoretical, thanks to the 'Wooden Walls of Old England'.

Nelson's War

THE WOODEN WALLS OF OLD ENGLAND

Napoleon's Grande Armée cut ruinous swathes across the whole of Europe. This self-elevated Emperor brought many nations to their knees. None could argue that on land this man at his peak was a ferocious and determined enemy sweeping all before him. On the sea a very different story was unfolding.

The Royal Navy, commanded by professional officers chosen for command because of their competence, had a worldwide and deserved reputation for being a solid and dependable wall of 'Heart of Oak' ships, surrounding an otherwise largely vulnerable island. This reputation did not come without a price. Discipline was extremely harsh and many of the sailors were virtual prisoners, unwilling pressed men who could be stripped of the skin of their backs by vicious flogging for a misdemeanour. However, this system worked. British gun crews, stooping in cramped, stinking, smoke-filled gundecks, raked by wooden splinters and deafened by the almost intolerable noise, could fire at over twice the rate of their French counterparts.

The attempted French blockade of British ports failed, whereas the British blockade of the French was very effective. Napoleon was unable to cross the few miles of water between Calais and Dover because he could not, even for a short time, quell the ships of His Majesty's Navy.

This war on the high seas culminated in Nelson's victory over the Franco-Spanish fleet off Cape Trafalgar on 21 October 1805. Other sea battles followed and Napoleon tried to rebuild his fleet, but the heart, physically and morally, had been torn out of the French navy.

HMS *Victory*, Nelson's flagship.

Ship's Crew

A seaman in 'shore-rig'. The hat was made of straw, which would be tarred in northern climates. Men purchased their own clothes, both shore-rig and working clothes. Generally the jacket was blue wool, although a uniform did not exist as such. A few ships' crew were dressed to the captain's taste.

The crew came from many social backgrounds. Some were professional seamen volunteering for service. . . .

. . . Others were 'pressed men' taken by force from towns, villages or even merchant ships. A continual flow of new men was required to replace those lost by enemy action or, more likely, disease and shipwreck.

Any male between the ages of eighteen and fifty-five was a target for the 'press gang' during a 'hot press', but normally the gang sought prime seamen.

Non-violent persuasion was the first recourse.

Violence was an underlying threat . . .

. . . and the ultimate persuasion. Press gangs were naturally very unpopular and the members were often set upon by the mob.

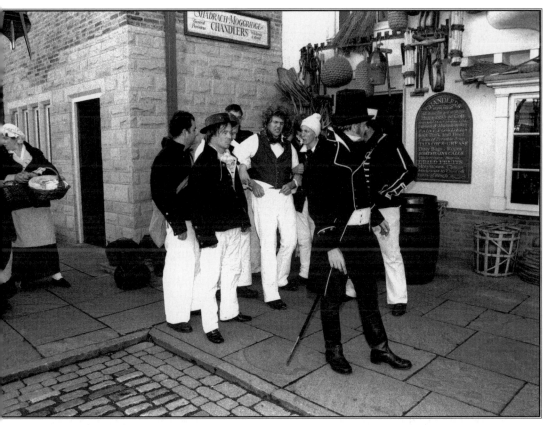

Men were torn away from family and the life they knew to the privations of sea life, a measure which is still legal.

Pressed men often spent many years at sea before they returned home.

Idlers were those whose general duties were subject to day duty and who therefore took no part in night watches. Each had his own skill that allowed him to escape the more rigorous duties of 'standing watch'. They included: Purser's assistant (pictured here), sailmakers and assistant carpenters.

Next in line of authority were the Petty Officers, who were appointed by the captain, and the Warrant Officers, appointed by the Admiralty or Navy Board. These included the Gunners. The gunner was a standing officer appointed to the ship and was a skilled man who understood mathematical principles and was responsible for all aspects of gunnery and maintenance.

The Master at Arms worked closely with the boatswain and his mates. He was a kind of policeman who kept an eye on impropriety in the crew. He also had the important task of seeing all fire and lights were out.

A Boatswain's Mate, one of the most feared men in the crew. They used their starters to 'persuade' men to work harder and administered floggings. Around his neck is the call (whistle) by which he sent orders around the ship.

Still higher in rank were those of Wardroom rank. They included the Purser, who was
financially responsible for the clothing and victuals and usually an educated man of some

personal wealth. Although most of his pay came from his financial dealings, a rather risky trade, there was never a shortage of applicants for the post.

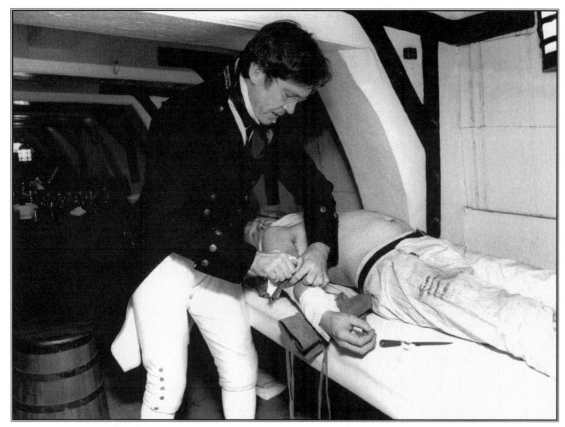

The Surgeon. In order to get the post, he simply had to pass an oral examination. However many of them were highly skilled and had medical degrees. Most of their work involved day-to-day health management of the crew, rather than the well-known gory aspects of amputation.

The Officers

The British Navy contained officers of the highest quality, often vastly superior in seamanship to their European counterparts. They reached their officer status by examination and experience at sea.

The First Lieutenant, the second in command on board. During any action he stood next to the captain ready to take over. On a small unrated vessel he would often be the commanding officer.

The first stage on the ladder of promotion to an officer was to become a Midshipman, usually after a period as 'Captain's servant' or 'Volunteer'. The volunteers were young boys and the midshipmen were usually in their twenties, but some were younger than fourteen. The midshipman was not an officer but an aspirant.

To rise to the next rank of Lieutenant a midshipman had to spend a minimum of six years at sea, two of which had to be as a midshipman, as well as passing an examination. This exam was usually conducted by a tribunal of captains. Here patronage and influence were important. Many midshipmen were men in their fifties who had not taken or passed the exam.

Lieutenants often stood watch and took the quarterdeck; however, the captain was called for major events, such as a change in the weather or sighting land.

The Royal Marines, 'Per Mare per Terram'. Given the title 'Royal' in 1802, the Royal Marines were the ship's military force and were subject to military training and discipline.

They acted as sharpshooters in close action, aiming for the enemy officers and gun crews.

They formed the core of landing parties.

It was not accidental that the
Royal Marines slept in quarters
between the crew and the officers,
affording not insubstantial
protection against mutiny.

At Trafalgar the Royal Marines suffered heavy casualties as a result of their exposed position on the upper deck.

Life at Sea

Discipline, harsh discipline, was essential for a group of men thrown together in cramped prison-like conditions, with few comforts other than a tot of rum.

Flogging was a standard punishment, administered in formal conditions with the ship's crew drawn up to watch the bloody spectacle.

The offender's crime was read out. He was allowed to defend himself. His officers were also invited to speak on his behalf. The captain then decided on the verdict and the number of lashes. If found guilty the offender would be strapped to an up-ended metal grating.

The whip was a length of rope separated into nine knotted lashes, the infamous 'Cat-o-nine-tails'. The wounds created by this vicious implement often exposed the white bones of the rib cage. An extreme and often fatal punishment of 'Flogging Round the Fleet' was employed for serious offenders such as mutineers. The luckless victim was rowed to each of the ships in the fleet where a set number of lashes were administered.

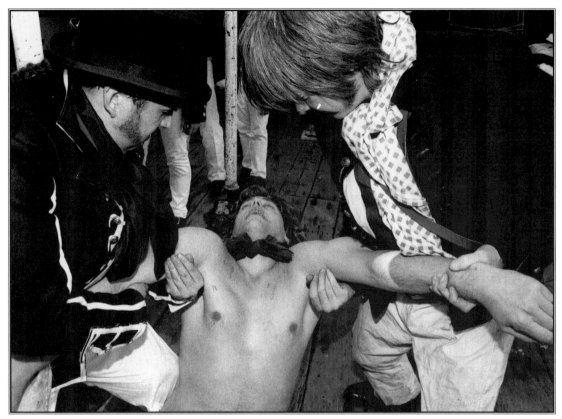

After completion of punishment the offender was taken down to the surgeon.

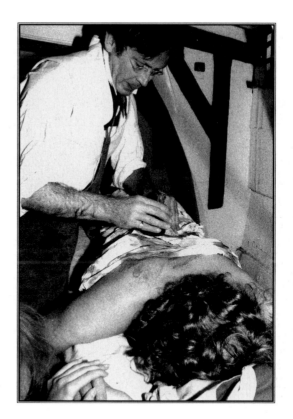

The wounds would be bound and
sterilized . . .

. . . with salt!

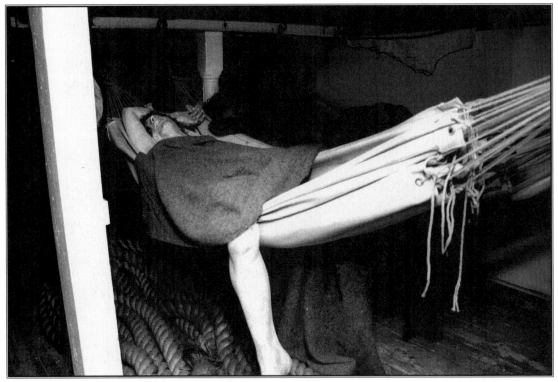

The hammock was a simple canvas sheet strung from the roof of the gun-decks. This basic arrangement provided a bed at night and during the day they would be stored on the upper deck where they would provide some degree of protection during enemy action.

The hammock might serve as a seamen's shroud but more usually an old piece of sailcloth would be used, with a cannonball sewn in so that the corpse would sink.

Food was adequate, if somewhat limited.

One contemporary record of a crew's daily food gives the following: Breakfast – Burgoo, made of coarse oatmeal and water, Scotch coffee, burnt bread boiled in water and sweetened with sugar; Noon – Grog ration of 1 gill of rum and three of water (one pint total) with sugar and lemon; Supper – Biscuits, cheese and butter. Nelson insisted that the men of his fleet were given onions or fruit to prevent the disease known as scurvy, an extremely unpleasant condition caused by a lack of vitamin C.

USEFUL ADDRESSES

Living History Photography

All the photographs in this book were taken by Paul Lewis Isemonger. These and thousands of others are available at reasonable cost for commercial or non-commercial use. Special low prices are available for schools and re-enactment groups. All pictures come fully captioned.
Living History Photography/
Photolibrary,
Park Wood House,
163 Thrupp Lane,
Far Thrupp,
Stroud,
Gloucestershire GL5 2EQ.
Tel. 01453 886140

'Sharpe's Peninsula' battlefield tours

March in the footsteps of Wellington's Army along with Rifleman Moore to the sites of victory in Portugal and Spain; and Waterloo.
Midas Tours,
Tel. 01883 744955.

Paul Meekins Military and History Books

For a large selection of new and secondhand books on the Napoleonic Wars and other periods from Roman to the Second World War. A mountain of reference books for this work were supplied by Paul Meekins, who provides an excellent and professional service. For a catalogue send two first-class stamps to:
34 Townsend Road,
Tiddington,
Stratford-upon-Avon,
Warks. CV37 7DE.
Tel. 01789 295086.

The Historic Art Company

The high-quality paintings of Chris Collingwood. Commissions undertaken for historically accurate paintings. Easily the best professional images of historical subjects I have seen. See *The Fighting Man* by Paul Lewis Isemonger and Chris Scott, published by Sutton Publishing.
4A Talfourd Ave,
Reading,
Berks. RG6 2BP.

Sarah Juniper, Cordwainer

Hand-made authentic boots and shoes. Exquisite museum-standard hand-made authentic shoes using traditional techniques. Highly recommended.
Tel. 01453 545675.

HMS *Trincomalee* Trust

For the preservation of the 1817 frigate HMS *Trincomalee* featured in this book.
Jackson Dock,
Hartlepool,
Cleveland TS24 0SQ.

Antique Newspapers

Specialists in newspapers 1665 to 1865. They supplied all newspaper references for this book. Very helpful.
PO Box 396,
Guernsey,
Channel Islands,
GY1 3FW.
Tel. 01481 712990.
Fax. 01481 725168.

Marcus Music

Manufacturers and suppliers of rope-tensioned drums, bodrans and tabors, plus other historical musical instruments.
S.a.e. for catalogue to:
Marcus Music,
Tredegar House,
Newport,
Gwent NP1 9YW.
Tel. 01633 815612.
Fax. 01633 816979.

The Living History Register Newsletter

Interesting articles on historical subjects, plus re-enactment events diary. A recent copy gave detailed instructions on how to construct a fifteenth-century bench and details of Victorian underpinnings, plus a short history of the English court jester.
Subscriptions to:
Pat Poppy and Roger Emmerson,
56 Wareham Road,
Lytchet Matravers,
Poole,
Dorset BH16 6DS.

Quartermasterie

Specialists in replica historical artefacts. A wide range of items in linen, horn, iron, tin, knitted wool, pottery, leather, pewter, glass, brass etc. High-quality items intended for re-enactment but worth collecting in their own right.
Ian Skipper,
Flat 1 Shelley Court,
4 Lovelace Road,
Surbiton,
Surrey KT6 6NP.

Pewter Replicas

Steve Millingham,
Church Tower Mint,
Hopton Cangeford,
Ludlow,
Shropshire. SY7 2EE.
Tel. 01584 823304

Albion Small Arms

Maker of fine reproduction muskets and guns. High quality craftsmanship
Ron Curley,
21 Green Lane,
Shelfield,
Walsall. WS4 1RN.
Tel. 01922 684964.

Past Tents

Reproduction tentage to suit any period, but specializing in Late Medieval English, American Civil War and Napoleonic designs.
A5 s.a.e. for catalogue to:
Past Tents,
Hill View Bungalow,
Main Street,

Clarborough,
Retford,
Notts. DN22 9NG.
Tel/Fax. 01777 869821.

Call to Arms

A listings and contact magazine for
most things connected with re-
enactment.
Call to Arms,
7 Chapmans Crescent,
Chesham,
Bucks HP5 2QU.
Tel. 01494 7484271.

English Heritage Special Events

The very best in re-enactment from
Romans and Celts to the Second
World War, small living history
events to huge displays of martial
skills, equipment and day-to-day life
in camp, as well as historical
entertainment and music/dance
events. All events are based in or
around an English Heritage
property. Highly recommended if
you want to see life as it really was.
Take your camera.
Special Events information line:
0171 973 3396.
For general enquiries on English
Heritage: 0171 973 3434.

St Dunstan's

Caring for men and women blinded
in the service of their country. They
need your help.
Contact: Neil M.J. Swan,
St Dunstan's – Room A7,
Freepost WD2,

12–14 Harcourt Street,
London W1A 4XB.

The Association of the Friends of Waterloo Committee

A worldwide charitable trust for the
study and research of the period,
based in the United Kingdom.
Secretary, John S. White,
2 Coburn Drive,
Four Oaks,
Sutton Coldfield B75 5NT.
Tel. 0121 3084103

High Definition Processing

Professional black-and-white
processing.
Avening Mill,
Avening,
Glos. GL8 8LU.
Tel. 01453 832889

Ages of Elegance

Makers of fine reproduction
uniforms and costume for men
and women. All periods. For
museums, re-enactments, film and
theatre.
Contact: Dawn Wood.
Tel. 0181 568 3210 or 0958 524936

The Plumery

The only manufacturers of
horsehair, feather and wool military
plumes in the world. No order too
small.
The Plumery,
16 Deans Close,
Whitehall Gardens,
Chiswick,
London W4 3LX.
Tel. 0181 995 7099.

RE-ENACTMENT GROUPS FEATURED IN THIS BOOK

The Historical Maritime Society

The only group re-enacting the Royal Navy and Royal Marines around the year 1805. Enlist now – avoid impressment!
Chris Jones,
3 Bell Hill,
Marton,
Lindal in Furness,
Ulverston,
Cumbria LA12 0NF.
Tel. 01229 463892.
e.mail. 75337.1362@
compuserve.com

9th (East Norfolk) Regiment of Foot
K. Phillips,
Plumtree Cottage,
Winslow Road,
Granborough,
Bucks. MK18 3NJ.

12th (Prince of Wales) Light Dragoons
M. Render,
Jasmine Cottage,
Fern Hill,
Nr. Glemsford,
Suffolk CU10 7PR.

15th or Kings Light Dragoons (Hussars)
Geoff Potts,
Calcot House,
Calcot Lane,
Curdridge,
Nr. Botley,
Southampton SO3 2BN.

42nd Royal Highland Regiment
Pipe Sergeant Walker,
Tel. 0181 505 3842.

95th (Rifles) Regiment of Foot
L. Handscombe,
48 Mutton Place,
Prince of Wales Road,
London NW1 8DF.

Military Music Re-enactors' Society
17 Booth Street,
Handsworth,
Birmingham B21 0NG.

21ème de Ligne
Chris Durkin,
22 Swallow Street,
Oldham,
Lancashire OL8 4LD.

1er Regiment de Chasseurs à Cheval de Ligne, 1er Escadron
Mike Grove,
Upper Woodhouse Farm,
Holmbridge,
West Yorks
HD7 1QR.

45ème de Ligne
David Prior,
29 Bayley Court,
Winnersh,
Wokingham,
Berkshire RG11 5HT.

Napoleonic Association
Chairman: Michael Freeman,
5 Thingwall Drive,
Irby,
Wirral,
Merseyside L61 3XN.